DOWNSIDE
OF DRUGS

Caffeine

Energy Drinks, Coffee, Soda, & Pills

DOWNSIDE of Drugs

ADHD Medication Abuse: Ritalin®, Adderall®, & Other Addictive Stimulants

Alcohol & Tobacco

Caffeine: Energy Drinks, Coffee, Soda, & Pills

Dangerous Depressants & Sedatives

Doping: Human Growth Hormone, Steroids, & Other Performance-Enhancing Drugs

Hard Drugs: Cocaine, LSD, PCP, & Heroin

Marijuana: Legal & Developmental Consequences

Methamphetamine & Other Amphetamines

New Drugs: Bath Salts, Spice, Salvia, & Designer Drugs

Over-the-Counter Medications

Prescription Painkillers: OxyContin®, Percocet®, Vicodin®, & Other Addictive Analgesics

DOWNSIDE OF DRUGS

Caffeine
Energy Drinks, Coffee, Soda, & Pills

Celicia Scott

Mason Crest

Mason Crest
450 Parkway Drive, Suite D
Broomall, PA 19008
www.masoncrest.com

Printed and bound in the United States of America.

First printing
9 8 7 6 5 4 3 2 1

Series ISBN: 978-1-4222-3015-2
Hardcover ISBN: 978-1-4222-3018-3
Paperback ISBN: 978-1-4222-3191-3
ebook ISBN: 978-1-4222-8804-7

Cataloging-in-Publication Data on file with the Library of Congress.

Contents

INTRODUCTION

One of the best parts of getting older is the opportunity to make your own choices. As your parents give you more space and you spend more time with friends than family, you are called upon to make more decisions for yourself. Many important decisions that present themselves in the teen years may change your life. The people with whom you are friendly, how much effort you put into school and other activities, and what kinds of experiences you choose for yourself all affect the person you will become as you emerge from being a child into becoming a young adult.

One of the most important decisions you will make is whether or not you use substances like alcohol, marijuana, crystal meth, and cocaine. Even using prescription medicines incorrectly or relying on caffeine to get through your daily life can shape your life today and your future tomorrow. These decisions can impact all the other decisions you make. If you decide to say yes to drug abuse, the impact on your life is usually not a good one!

One suggestion I make to many of my patients is this: think about how you will respond to an offer to use drugs before it happens. In the heat of the moment, particularly if you're feeling some peer pressure, it can be hard to think clearly—so be prepared ahead of time. Thinking about why you don't want to use drugs and how you'll respond if you are asked to use them can make it easier to make a healthy decision when the time comes. Just like practicing a sport makes it easier to play in a big game, having thought about why drugs aren't a good fit for you and exactly what you might say to avoid them can give you the "practice" you need to do what's best for you. It can make a tough situation simpler once it arises.

In addition, talk about drugs with your parents or a trusted adult. This will both give you support and help you clarify your thinking. The decision is still yours to make, but adults can be a good resource. Take advantage of the information and help they can offer you.

Sometimes, young people fall into abusing drugs without really thinking about it ahead of time. It can sometimes be hard to recognize when you're making a decision that might hurt you. You might be with a friend or acquaintance in a situation that feels comfortable. There may be things in your life that are hard, and it could seem like using drugs might make them easier. It's also natural to be curious about new experiences. However, by not making a decision ahead of time, you may be actually making a decision without realizing it, one that will limit your choices in the future.

When someone offers you drugs, there is no flashing sign that says, "Hey, think about what you're doing!" Making a good decision may be harder because the "fun" part happens immediately while the downside—the damage to your brain and the rest of your body—may not be obvious right away. One of the biggest downsides of drugs is that they have long-term effects on your life. They could reduce your educational, career, and relationship opportunities. Drug use often leaves users with more problems than when they started.

Whenever you make a decision, it's important to know all the facts. When it comes to drugs, you'll need answers to questions like these: How do different drugs work? Is there any "safe" way to use drugs? How will drugs hurt my body and my brain? If I don't notice any bad effects right away, does that mean these drugs are safe? Are these drugs addictive? What are the legal consequences of using drugs? This book discusses these questions and helps give you the facts to make good decisions.

Reading this book is a great way to start, but if you still have questions, keep looking for the answers. There is a lot of information on the Internet, but not all of it is reliable. At the back of this book, you'll find a list of more books and good websites for finding out more about this drug. A good website is teens.drugabuse.gov, a site compiled for teens by the National Institute on Drug Abuse (NIDA). This is a reputable federal government agency that researches substance use and how to prevent it. This website does a good job looking at a lot of data and consolidating it into easy-to-understand messages.

What if you are worried you already have a problem with drugs? If that's the case, the best thing to do is talk to your doctor or another trusted adult to help figure out what to do next. They can help you find a place to get treatment.

Drugs have a downside—but as a young adult, you have the power to make decisions for yourself about what's best for you. Use your power wisely!

—Joshua Borus, MD

1. WHAT IS CAFFEINE?

When you hear the word "caffeine," the next word that comes into your head is probably "coffee." Many people in the world get their caffeine from coffee—but it's also found in many other foods, drinks, and medicines. Caffeine is a drug. And it has a downside.

A drug is any chemical that changes the way your body works. Drugs can do good things—like medicines that cure diseases or take away pain. Drugs can also do bad things to your body—like heroin, cocaine, and other street drugs. Sometimes a drug that is harmless or **beneficial** in small doses can be very dangerous in larger does.

Caffeine is a kind of drug called a stimulant. Stimulants speed up your nervous system. They make you feel excited and alert and full of energy. This sounds like a good thing—but stimulants can be dangerous.

Caffeine is also a psychoactive drug. This means that it's a chemical that crosses the **blood-brain barrier**. It gets inside the brain and the **central nervous system**. It changes the way the brain works.

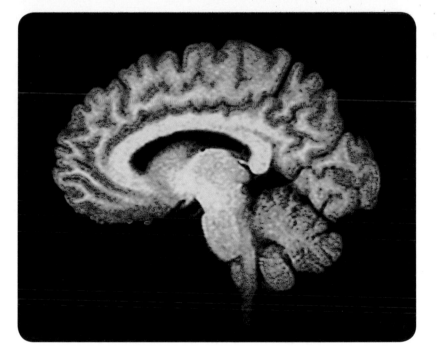

Caffeine

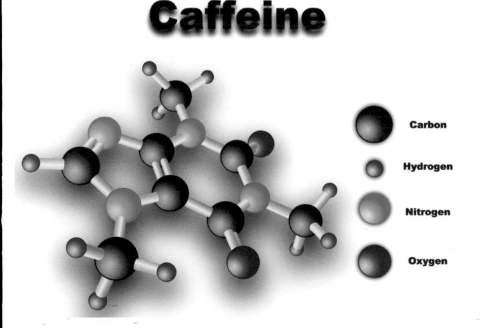

Carbon

Hydrogen

Nitrogen

Oxygen

Caffeine is actually a chemical that's made up of atoms of carbon, oxygen, nitrogen, and hydrogen.

WHAT'S THE DOWNSIDE OF CAFFEINE?

Researchers are looking into caffeine. Is it good for us? Is it bad for us? Scientists are discovering that caffeine may be more dangerous than people think. It has many short-term effects on your body, including your brain. It also has long-term effects that can cause serious illnesses.

Caffeine interferes with the way your body absorbs the vitamins and minerals it needs to be healthy. It can make your body lose the fluids it needs to function well. It can make you feel nervous and anxious. It can cause headaches and stomach aches.

Caffeine isn't just a "pick-me-up." When it makes your brain and body feel energized, it also triggers the release of stress hormones. Stress is how we respond to difficult things in our lives. Our bodies react to get us ready for whatever we have to face. Caffeine does the same thing, even though there's no real challenge in front of us. So we're stressed out for no reason! And too much stress is bad for us, physically and emotionally.

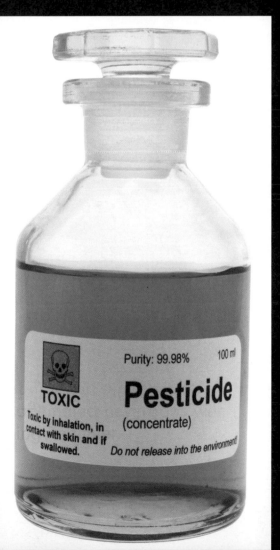

It's very likely that your coffee beans have been exposed to pesticides. Pesticides are chemicals intended to kill insects and other pests on crops. When you eat these chemicals, though, they can cause cancer.

3. WHAT HAPPENS INSIDE YOUR BODY WHEN YOU USE CAFFEINE?

Caffeine is absorbed through the lining of your stomach and small intestine. When it reaches your brain, it changes the way chemicals called neurotransmitters work. This can make you feel more perky—but it can also make you feel shaky and stressed out.

There are tiny gaps between the nerve cells in your brain, and neurotransmitters help nerve cells pass messages across these gaps. Neurotransmitters have an important job. When they do their job right, you feel happy. You can handle anything that comes your way. When these chemicals are out of whack, though, you can feel sad or nervous or tense.

Caffeine reaches the bloodstream about 45 minutes after it's consumed, so it takes that long before you can expect to feel its effects. Your blood carries caffeine to your brain and also throughout your entire body.

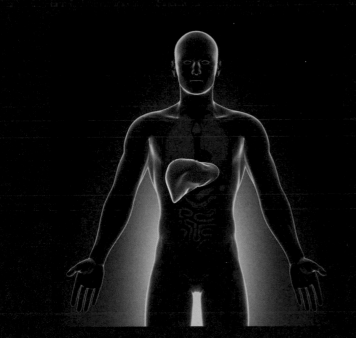

Eventually, your liver will break down the caffeine and turn it into other chemicals. These chemicals also have effects on your body. They make your blood vessels *dilate*, which increases blood pressure. They make you produce more urine than usual.

Finally, the caffeine's chemicals pass through your kidneys and leave your body through your urine. After about 5 hours, half of the caffeine you consumed will be out of your body—but it takes a full 24 hours before it's totally gone. This means you may be feeling caffeine's effect nearly a day after you drank your last cup of coffee!

4. WHERE DOES CAFFEINE COME FROM?

Caffeine is found in at least 60 plants. It acts as a natural pesticide, killing certain insects that try to eat the plants.

Coffee beans are the world's most common source of caffeine. Caffeine is also in tea leaves, cocoa nuts, and the kola nut.

Caffeine was first used by Stone Age people who got it from chewing on bark, plants, and seeds. They probably noticed that when they chewed certain trees and plants, they felt more alert and had more energy. Ancient Native Americans drank something they called "Black Drink," which also contained caffeine.

R. Saturjona

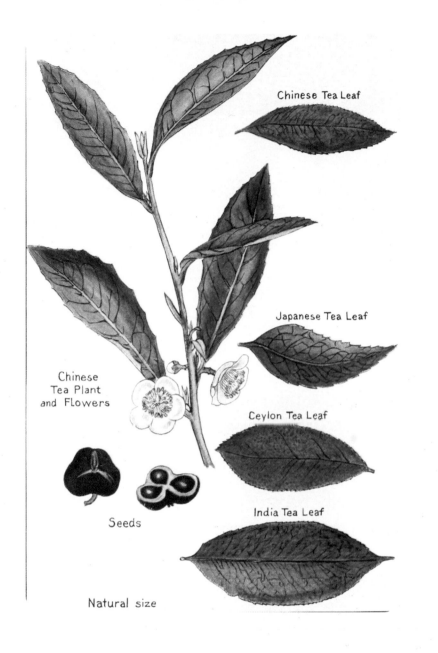

Chinese Tea Leaf

Japanese Tea Leaf

Chinese
Tea Plant
and Flowers

Ceylon Tea Leaf

Seeds

India Tea Leaf

Natural size

Tea leaves have about half as much caffeine as coffee beans. Tea first grew in China. According to one legend, 5,000 years ago the emperor of China accidentally discovered that when some tea leaves fell into boiling water, it made a fragrant and energizing drink. Explorers in the 1600s brought tea to Europe, where it soon became a favorite drink.

Cocoa beans were first grown on trees like this in Mexico and Central America, long before Europeans arrived on the scene. Nearly 3,000 years ago, the Maya drank a hot, spicy chocolate drink that was thought to fight tiredness. The Spanish explorers brought chocolate back to Europe in the 1600s.

One of the ingredients in Coca-Cola used to be kola, a nut that comes from Africa. People there have chewed it for thousands of years to relieve hunger pangs and restore energy levels.

17

5. WHY DO PEOPLE USE CAFFEINE?

Caffeine drinks like coffee and tea have become a part of everyday life. People start their days with a cup of coffee or tea. They drink caffeine drinks while they take a break during their workdays. They sip them when they get together to talk with friends. They have a cup after dinner. Caffeine drinks are connected in people's minds with comfort and good times.

But people also drink caffeine drinks to give them energy and wake them up. Sometimes they use caffeine to make them stay awake when they would normally be sleeping. Students who want to stay up all night studying often drink a lot of coffee or take caffeine in some other form.

Some of the first people who drank coffee were monks in Ethiopia. They drank it so they could stay awake better during their prayers.

Coffee houses were first opened in Europe during the 1600s. People got together there to sip coffee and talk. Today coffee shops are still popular places to meet friends. In fact, one of the most popular coffee shops in the world, Starbucks, has opened on average two new shops every day since 1987!

The world drinks about 120,000 tons of caffeine every year. That's equal to one serving of caffeine for every person every day. This makes it the world's most popular drug!

19

6. HOW DO PEOPLE GET CAFFEINE?

In North America, most people get their caffeine from coffee beverages. In other parts of the world, tea is more common. Soft drinks and medicines also contain caffeine, and so do some candies. Energy drinks also contain lots of caffeine.

In North America, 90 percent of adults consume some amount of caffeine daily.

Different kinds of coffee contain different amounts of caffeine. In general, a serving of coffee contains somewhere between 40 and 100 milligrams of coffee. Dark roasts have less than lighter roasts because the roasting process reduces the beans' caffeine content.

Tea usually contains about half as much caffeine per serving as coffee, depending on the strength of the brew. Certain types of tea, such as black and oolong, contain somewhat more caffeine than most other teas.

Soft drinks usually contain about 10 to 50 milligrams of caffeine per serving.

Energy drinks like Red Bull have about 80 milligrams of caffeine per serving.

7. HOW DOES CAFFEINE MAKE YOU FEEL?

At first, caffeine makes you feel good. You may feel happier and full of energy after your morning cup of coffee. But that good feeling won't last.

When you drink a cup of your favorite caffeinated beverage, it triggers your body to release a chemical called adrenaline. Adrenaline is the chemical that gets you ready for "fight or flight." Your muscles, your eyes, all your body organs, and your brain are ready to either fight something—or run as fast as you can in the opposite direction. Your brain doesn't need to do much thinking, so more oxygen gets sent to your heart (allowing it to beat faster) and your muscles (so they get ready to either fight or run), while not so much is sent to your brain cells. This is great if there's a bear chasing you—but not so great if you've just drank a cup of coffee and now you have to go school. When caffeine puts your brain and body into this state, your emotions are more likely to take charge. It's harder for your brain to think and learn.

Feeling grouchy and anxious are the most common emotional effects of caffeine—but researchers have found that caffeine lets ALL your emotions to take charge. So any emotional reaction you have is likely to be stronger.

Caffeine may give your mood a short-term lift—but that lift wears off quickly. When that happens, people may reach for another cup of coffee. Many people have become **dependent** on multiple caffeine fixes throughout their days.

The chemical in caffeine changes the way your brain works because it's a lot like another chemical called adenosine. Adenosine is a brain chemical that causes drowsiness by slowing down nerve cell activity. *Receptors* in your brain cells normally bind with adenosine—but when caffeine comes along, they bind with it instead. Now adenosine can't do its job. Your nerve cells keep firing. You stay alert instead of getting sleepy.

AND WHAT DOES IT DO TO THE REST OF YOUR BODY?

The **pituitary gland** senses all the activity going on in your brain. It thinks some sort of emergency must be occurring—so it releases hormones that tell the **adrenal glands** to produce adrenaline.

Adrenaline is the "fight-or-flight" hormone. It does a bunch of things to your body:

- Your pupils dilate.
- The airways in your lungs open up wider.
- Your heart beats faster.
- Blood vessels near your skin **constrict** to slow blood flow to your skin (in case you get injured in the "fight").
- Blood flow to the muscles of your arms and legs increases.
- Your blood pressure rises.
- Blood flow to your stomach slows, which may cause indigestion.
- The liver releases sugar into the bloodstream for extra energy.
- Your muscles tighten, ready for action.

So if you drink a big cup of coffee, you may find your hands get cold, your muscles grow tense, you feel excited, and your heart beats faster.

25

9. HOW CAN CAFFEINE MAKE YOU SICK?

A cup of coffee a day probably isn't going to make you sick. But if you consume a lot of caffeine every day, day after day, it's not good for you. Eventually, it can cause a variety of health conditions. These range from uncomfortable to life threatening.

Caffeine is hard on the lining of your stomach and intestines. Especially in some people, it can cause cramps and diarrhea. It can also make you more likely to get an *ulcer*.

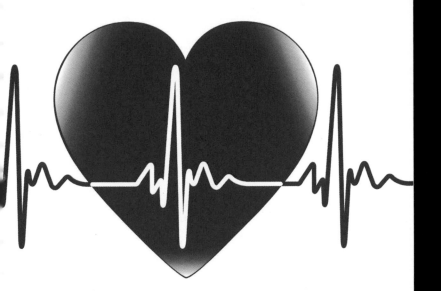

Too much caffeine may be bad for your heart. It can make your heartbeat **irregular** and fluttery. Researchers have also found that for some people, two or more cups of coffee a day can increase their risk of heart disease.

Too much caffeine can make your bones weak. As you get older, you'll be more likely to break bones.

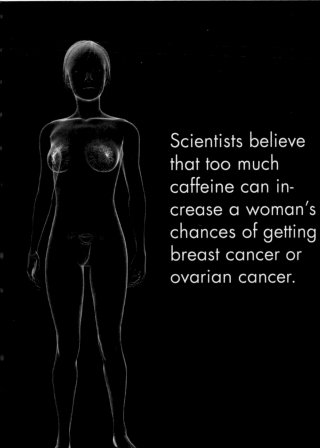

Scientists believe that too much caffeine can increase a woman's chances of getting breast cancer or ovarian cancer.

Caffeine can cause headaches.

27

10. IS CAFFEINE ADDICTIVE?

If you consume a lot of caffeine, your body will come to depend on it. This means it needs caffeine in order to function normally. The more caffeine you consume, the more you will want to consume it. If you're addicted, quitting caffeine will be difficult.

If you're used to consuming a lot of caffeine and you try to quit or cut back, you'll probably feel tired and headachy. You may feel anxious and sad. It may be hard to concentrate. You might feel grumpy. Some people feel achy all over when they quit caffeine, and some have nausea or vomiting.

Withdrawal symptoms won't last forever, though! You'll probably start to feel bad about 12 to 24 hours after your last caffeine fix. Symptoms can last from 2 to 9 days. After that, you'll no longer crave caffeine. You'll be ready for a healthier lifestyle! You can replace all those caffeinated beverages with something healthier.

11. HOW DOES CAFFEINE AFFECT YOUR SLEEP?

You drink a cup of coffee when you need to wake up, right? But sleep experts tell us that actually that cup of coffee may make you sleepier in the long run. That's because caffeine can interfere with your body's normal sleep patterns. Researchers have found that people who have a daily intake of caffeine are more likely to have both nighttime sleep problems and daytime sleepiness.

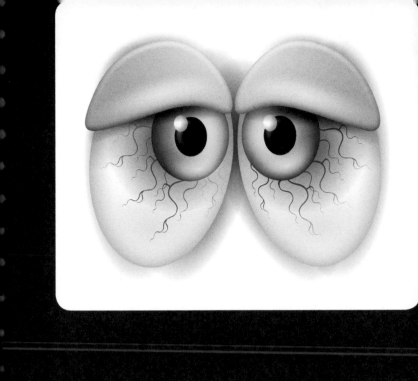

Caffeine drinkers are more likely to wake up often during the night. They sleep less soundly and deeply.

Researchers found that about 33 percent of teenagers fall asleep during the day. Most of these kids consume caffeine daily, while most of the 76 percent who do not fall asleep during the day do not consume caffeine.

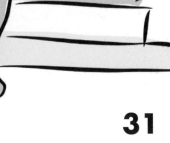

Experts don't agree on how much caffeine is safe to consume and how much is too much. A 2014 study by the Mayo Clinic, however, found that adults under fifty-five who drank more than 28 eight-ounce cups of coffee (on average, 4 cups of coffee a day) had a 55 percent increased risk of dying.

Another study, this one done by Swiss scientists, found that teenagers who drink more than 3 cups of coffee, 3 cans of energy drink, or one large bottle of cola a day may be damaging their brains' abilities to develop normally.

One eight-ounce cup of a caffeinated beverage a day probably won't hurt you. More than that could.

Unlike many other psycho-active drugs, caffeine is legal. No laws tell you how much you can consume.

Main symptoms of
Caffeine overdose

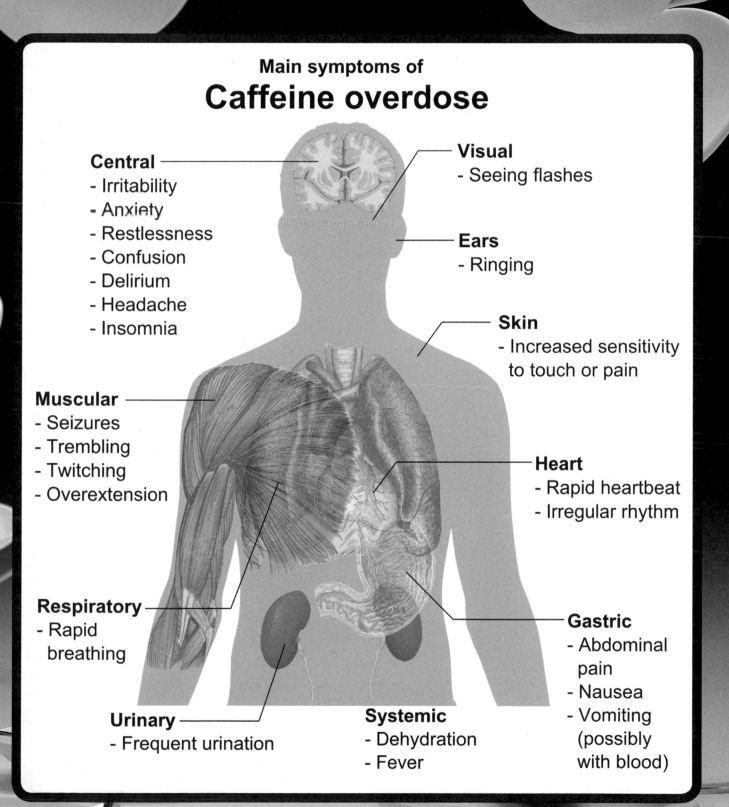

Central
- Irritability
- Anxiety
- Restlessness
- Confusion
- Delirium
- Headache
- Insomnia

Visual
- Seeing flashes

Ears
- Ringing

Skin
- Increased sensitivity to touch or pain

Muscular
- Seizures
- Trembling
- Twitching
- Overextension

Heart
- Rapid heartbeat
- Irregular rhythm

Respiratory
- Rapid breathing

Urinary
- Frequent urination

Systemic
- Dehydration
- Fever

Gastric
- Abdominal pain
- Nausea
- Vomiting (possibly with blood)

13. SHOULD I MIX CAFFEINE AND SPORTS?

Some athletes believe that caffeine helps them perform better. Experts say that caffeine's affects may in fact give athletes a temporary boost. However, many sports organizations, including the Olympics committee and the NCAA, are starting to ban caffeine. They say that because caffeine ISN'T regulated, people aren't always aware of how much they're drinking—and that can make exercise and caffeine a dangerous combination.

In 2000, an Irish basketball player died after drinking several cans of Red Bull after a game.

In 2000, an Astros pitcher was hospitalized for **dehydration** after drinking several cans of Red Bull.

When you're exercising, it's especially important to drink lots of water and stay **hydrated**! Caffeine makes you pee more, and this can mean your cells have less of the water they need.

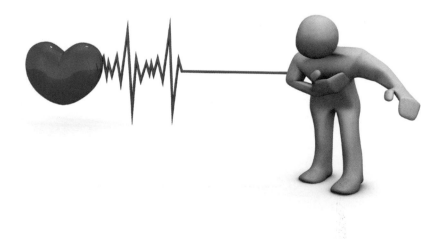

Caffeine can make your heartbeat irregular—and you need your heart at peak performance during exercise.

14. DOES CAFFEINE CHANGE HOW WELL YOU DO IN SCHOOL?

You might think that a cup of coffee is just what you need to keep you alert during a boring class. Or you may guzzle an energy drink to help you stay awake for studying during finals week. But actually, caffeine consumption has been linked to students not doing as well in school. Scientists suspect that caffeine may affect your ability to remember and learn. Caffeine also interferes with your sleep schedule—and sleepy brains don't learn as well!

A 2007 sleep study found that teenagers who consume caffeine regularly are more likely to miss school and have lower grade-point averages than kids who don't consume caffeine.

A 2003 study found that young adults who consume caffeine are more likely to be sleepy or fall asleep while at school.

Another study found that kids who consumed caffeine were more likely to feel anxious and experience "test anxiety."

15.

CAFFEINE CONTENT PER SERVING IN MILLIGRAMS

Coffee, Brewed	80–135
Red Bull	80
Ben & Jerry's Coffee Fudge Frozen Yogurt (8oz)	85
Coffee, Instant	65–100
Tea, iced	47
Tea, brewed, imported brands	60
Tea, brewed, U.S. brands	40
Tea, instant	30
Tea, green	15
Hot cocoa	14
Coffee, Decaf, brewed	3–4
Coffee, Decaf, instant	2–3
Dark chocolate (1 oz)	20
Diet Dr. Pepper	41
Diet Sunkist Orange	41
Mr. Pibb	40
Sugar-Free Mr. Pibb	40
Red Flash	40
Sunkist Orange	40

Storm	38
Big Red	38
Pepsi-Cola	37.5
Diet Pepsi	36
Aspen	36
Coca-Cola Classic	34
Snapple Flavored Teas	31.5
Canada Dry Cola	30
A&W Creme Soda	29
Nestea Sweet Iced Tea	26
Barq's Root Beer	23
A&W Diet Creme Soda	22
Snapple Sweet Tea	12
Lipton Brisk, All Varieties	9
Canada Dry Diet Cola	1.2
Diet Rite Cola	0
Sprite	0
7-Up	0
A&W Root Beer	0
Slice	0
Sierra Mist	0
Fresca	0

What are some hidden sources of caffeine?

- Coffee ice cream has caffeine—about 30 milligrams in a half-cup.
- Weight-loss pills have caffeine too. Caffeine doesn't actually make you lose weight, but it may make you less aware of your hunger. Some diet pills contain as much caffeine as 12 cups of coffee!
- Some over-the-counter painkillers contain caffeine.
- "Energy waters" usually contain caffeine.
- Some breath fresheners contain caffeine.
- Any food that claims to give you energy—from oatmeal to beef jerky—probably contains caffeine. Check the label to be safe!

Could caffeine kill you?

Deaths from caffeine overdose are rare, but they do happen. The amount of caffeine considered to be an overdose varies by a person's size, age and gender. In general, doses of greater than 10 grams will be fatal in adults.

Can caffeine harm an unborn baby?

Experts say pregnant women should limit their caffeine intake. Some studies have linked a high intake of caffeine to increased risk for *miscarriage* and babies who don't grow normally.

Does caffeine counteract the affects of alcohol?

This is a common myth—but it's not true! Caffeine does absolutely nothing to counteract alcohol's affects. If you're drunk and you drink 5 cups of black coffee, you'll still be drunk! (But you'll probably have to pee quite a bit.)

FURTHER READING

Allen, Stewart Lee. *The Devil's Cup: A History of the World According to Coffee.* New York: Ballantine, 2003.

Cherniske, Stephen. *Caffeine Blues: Wake Up to the Dangers of America's #1 Drug.* New York: Warner, 2008.

Hasan, Heather. *Caffeine and Nicotine: A Dependent Society.* New York: Rosen, 2009.

Kaplan. *Caffeine Will Not Help You Pass That Test.* New York: Kaplan, 2005.

Klosterman, Lorrie. *The Facts About Caffeine.* Salt Lake City, Ut.: Benchmarck, 2006.

Kushner, Marina. *The Truth About Caffeine.* New York: SCR, 2011.

Marcowitz, Hall. *Caffeine.* Farmington Hills, Mich.: Lucent, 2006.

Weinberg, Bennet Alan. *The World of Caffeine: The Science and Culture of the World's Most Popular Drug.* New York: Routledge, 2001.

FIND OUT MORE ON THE INTERNET

Biology Case Studies: Caffeine and the Brain
www.mhhe.com/biosci/genbio/casestudies/narcolepsy.mhtml

Caffeine and Kids
healthycanadians.gc.ca/kids-enfants/food-aliment/drinks-boissons-eng.php

Generation C: Is Caffeine the Next Kids' Health Crisis
www.foxnews.com/health/2013/01/28/generation-c-is-caffeine-next-kids-health-crisis

Healthy U: Caffeine and Kids
www.healthyalberta.com/1164.htm

How Stuff Works: Caffeine
science.howstuffworks.com/caffeine4.htm

Kids' Health: Caffeine
kidshealth.org/teen/food_fitness/nutrition/caffeine.html

Neuroscience for Kids: Caffeine
faculty.washington.edu/chudler/caff.html

GLOSSARY

adrenal glands: The parts of your body that make adrenaline, found right above your kidneys.

beneficial: Good for your health in some way.

blood-brain barrier: A filter that keeps certain chemicals in your blood from getting into your brain.

cancer: A disease where cells in your body multiply out of control.

central nervous system: Your brain and spinal cord, which work together to control your entire body.

constrict: To squeeze and get smaller.

dehydration: When your body doesn't have enough water to function correctly.

dependent: Needing something to survive or function.

dilate: When something circular like your pupils or blood vessels gets larger.

hormones: Chemicals that control how your body develops and how you feel.

hydrated: Having enough water in your body.

irregular: Uneven.

miscarriage: An embryo or fetus that dies before it is born.

pituitary gland: A gland in your brain that controls many different functions in your body, including how quickly you grow.

receptors: The parts of cells that chemicals like hormones and neurotransmitters attach to.

researchers: Scientists who study new things and make new discoveries.

ulcer: A sore inside your stomach.

withdrawal symptoms: The negative effects you feel when you stop taking a drug that your body is dependent on.

INDEX

PICTURE CREDITS

ABOUT THE AUTHOR
AND THE CONSULTANT

CELICIA SCOTT lives in upstate New York. She worked in teaching before starting a second career as a writer.

JACK E. HENNINGFIELD, Ph.D., is a professor at the Johns Hopkins University School of Medicine, and he is also Vice President for Research and Health Policy at Pinney Associates, a consulting firm in Bethesda, Maryland, that specializes in science policy and regulatory issues concerning public health, medications development, and behavior-focused disease management. Dr. Henningfield has contributed information relating to addiction to numerous reports of the U.S. Surgeon General, the National Academy of Sciences, and the World Health Organization.